Dear Danny, Beaty,
Emma and Tom,
thank you for your
wonderful hospitality. May this book
should be a constant reminder of
Yotvat and yoKam, and the beauty of
the Desert.

מפרץ השלום,
8 באוגוסט, 1994

Peace Fleet,
Eilat Bay
8 August, 1994

DESERT'S EDGE

SKYLINE – EILOT REGION

DESERT'S EDGE

SKYLINE – EILOT REGION

Photography: DUBY TAL
Piloting: MONI HARAMATI

Editing:
DUBY TAL, HANAN GINAT, VARDA RAZ DE MIRANDA

Design: VARDA RAZ DE MIRANDA

Photographs on pages no. 98, 135 – DAVID NETAH

Texts:
RONY MALKA
BENJAMIN SHALMON
SHLOMO TUSHINSKY
ASSAF HOLZER
HANAN GINAT

© The rights for the song on page 4
belongs to JONATHAN GEFEN or ACUM

English Translation: THE WRITE STUFF LTD.

The maps were printed with permission by
The Survey of Israel
and the Ministry of Tourism

Satellite Photograph:
© 1994. Rohr Productions Ltd. C.N.E.S.

Production: ALBATROSS – AERIAL PHOTOGRAPHY LTD.
Production Supervision: MONI HARAMATI, VARDA RAZ DE MIRANDA

Typesetting: EL-OT LTD.
Color Separation: GRAPH-OR LTD.
Plates, Printing & Production Assistance: KAL PRESS LTD.
Binding by: KETER PRESS, JERUSALEM

Printed in Israel 1994

ISBN 965-222-572-X

The authors wish to thank:
ALFONSO NUSSBAUMER and BOAZ PELEG
for their assistance

Albatross – Aerial Photography Ltd.

ALBATROSS

Eilot Regional Council

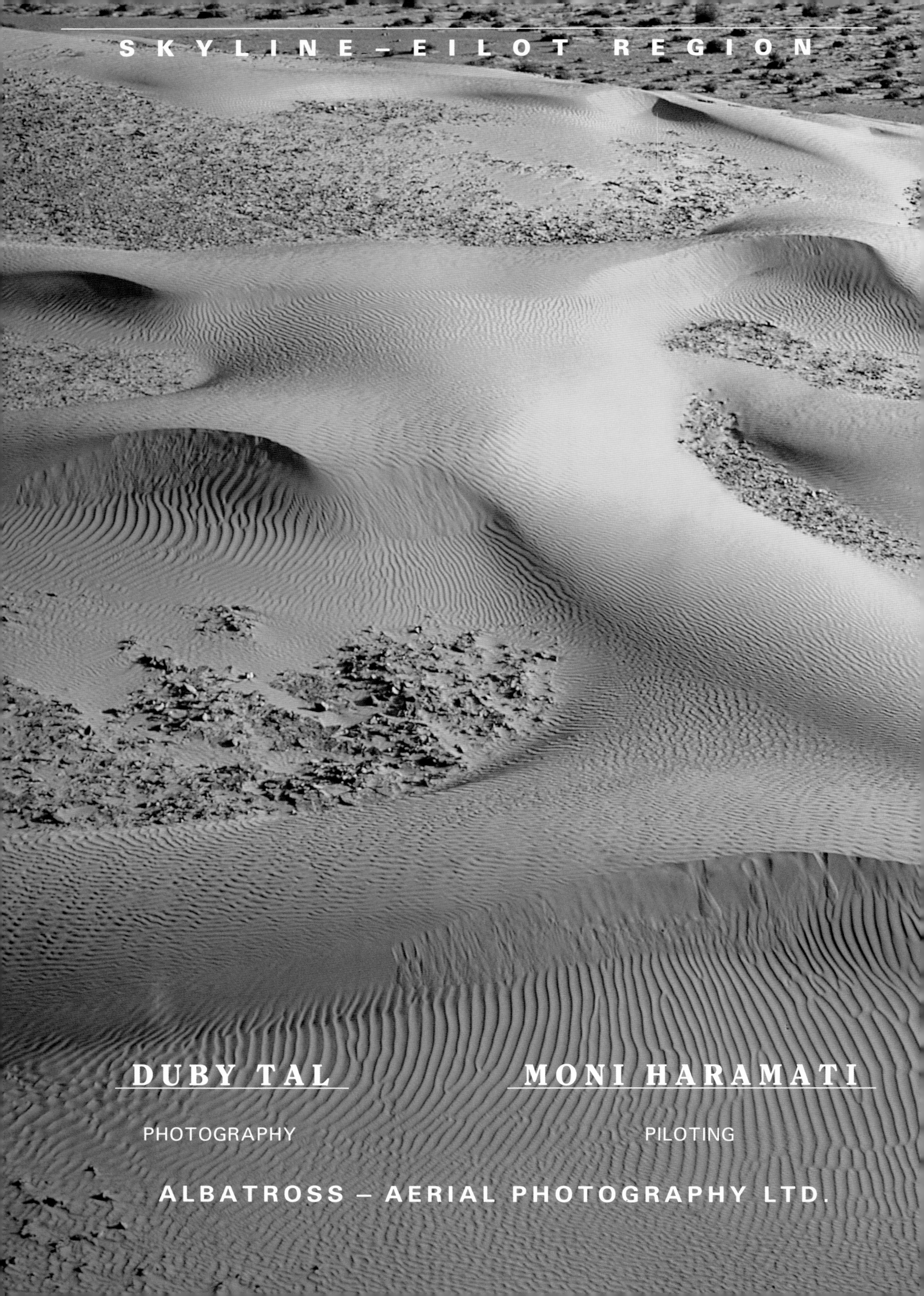

SKYLINE – EILOT REGION

DUBY TAL

PHOTOGRAPHY

MONI HARAMATI

PILOTING

ALBATROSS – AERIAL PHOTOGRAPHY LTD.

DESERT'S EDGE

CONTENTS

After first visiting Eilat in 1935. David Ben-Gurion wrote a memorandum to U.S. Supreme Court Judge Louis Brandeis, one of America's leading Zionists. In it he depicted the lush land of the southern Arava Valley and suggested settling a group of one hundred pioneers in the area to cultivate its fertile soil. In 1950. the cadet corps (Gadna) founded a youth village named Beer Ora near Bir Hindis (Arabic for "the well of death"), the only source of water in the area. That same year, the Israel Labor Party started a youth movement called "Shahal" ("The Israeli Pioneer Service.") Its first group settled in Evrona and conducted agricultural experiments. Shahal also started another colony in Ras El Naqb. called Ein Netafim. These settlements were disbanded after a short time.

Thanks to the discovery of water in Ein Radian. "Nahal" founded Nahlaim-3. In 1957. they proceeded to found Yotvata. the first kibbutz in the southern Arava Valley. Five years later, Kibbutz Eilot was established near Eilat. by a group previously employed in building the Eilat port and its fishing industry.

In 1964, the Eilot regional council was established in the southern Negev and Arava Valley region. Two years later, the council's territory tripled in size to 815 thousand acres; in 1976. the northern part of the council's tract was reassigned to the local council of the middle Arava Valley.

In 1966. the Nahal settlement Gerofit became a civilian community; in the seventies. three new kibbutzim – Qetura (1973). Samar (1976) and Yahel (1977). were founded. These were followed by the kibbutzim of Shizafon (1982. and eventually resettled in 1989 by a group which changed the name to Neot Smadar), Lotan (1983). Eliphaz (1983). Newe Harif (1985) and the community settlement of Ma'ale Shaharut. By then the population of the council's communities had grown to 2,500.

Shlomo Tuschinski (Tushi)

Chairman of Eilot Region Council

From the first days of Israeli statehood, the southern Arava has represented a challenge for the Jewish Agency. Its Settlement Department concentrated most of its efforts on the region and assigned its best workers to aid pioneers who had established the first settlements in this distant district.

Every settlement and factory in the southern Arava was established through the aid of the Jewish Agency. Along with developing production means, the Agency is involved in absorbing new settlers, creating a quality lifestyle and establishing a socio-educational foundation.

Due its authoritative role as a trustee of Jewish communities around the world, the Jewish Agency employs financial aid to establish and strengthen settlements. The connection between settlers, their settlement movements and Diaspora Jewry has allowed the Jewish Agency to act as a bridge builder, creating bonds of sympathy between Jews around the world identifying with the goals and faith of southern Arava settlers. The fruits of these efforts can be seen the length of the road leading south, towards Eilat.

Despite difficulties arising from the Eilot region's location, the Arava's population is growing and its settlements are flourishing.

With the beginning of the "Partnership 2,000" factory the Department for Rural and Urban Development has taken upon itself the task of intensifying Arava settlement relations with Toronto Jewry and other Jewish communities. This is being done at a time when the dream of peace is turning into a reality.

As an interested party involved in the Eilot region's development, the Jewish Agency invites you to join Eilot settlers in the story of their success.

Yigal Yerushalmi

The Jewish Agency For Israel
Department For Rural and Urban Development

THE LARGE WADIS

For millions of years, the waters of what now are Paran and Zihor wadis ran into the Dead Sea, draining the Negev's southwestern region, creating a smooth stone wilderness. Vertical rock layers, kilometers long, testify to a continuous breaking and wrinkling of land even far from the Arava. Wide, medium range mountains, such as Mt. Karkom, Mt. Zenifim, Mt. Hallamish and Mt. Zur'az, loom over these areas.

The abundance of fossils testifies to the area's rich past of fresh water lakes and rainfall. As a result of decreased rainfall over thousands of years, the present-day desert climate emerged.

Despite the area's arid nature, annual and perennial vegetation can still be found along main water channels. Towering acacia trees – some of them hundreds of years old – and tall bushes, such as Desert Broom, benefit from an improved water supply along the rivers. Small water pools and animal life, including wild asses, gazelles, mountain goats, hyenas, wolves, cats, foxes, fowl and reptiles, also exists in these barren areas. Brimming pools of water, full after a flood, are sources of relief for larger animals. This astounding ecological balance, within which there is little human interference, represents one of the unique focuses of the Nature Reserve in southern Israel.

Hundreds of archaeological sites, including several burial spots, can be found in this region. An unusually large concentration of rock engravings, animal shapes formed out of small stones and human relics are scattered along Mt. Karkom. Some scholars believe that Mt. Karkom is the mysterious, biblical Mt. Sinai.

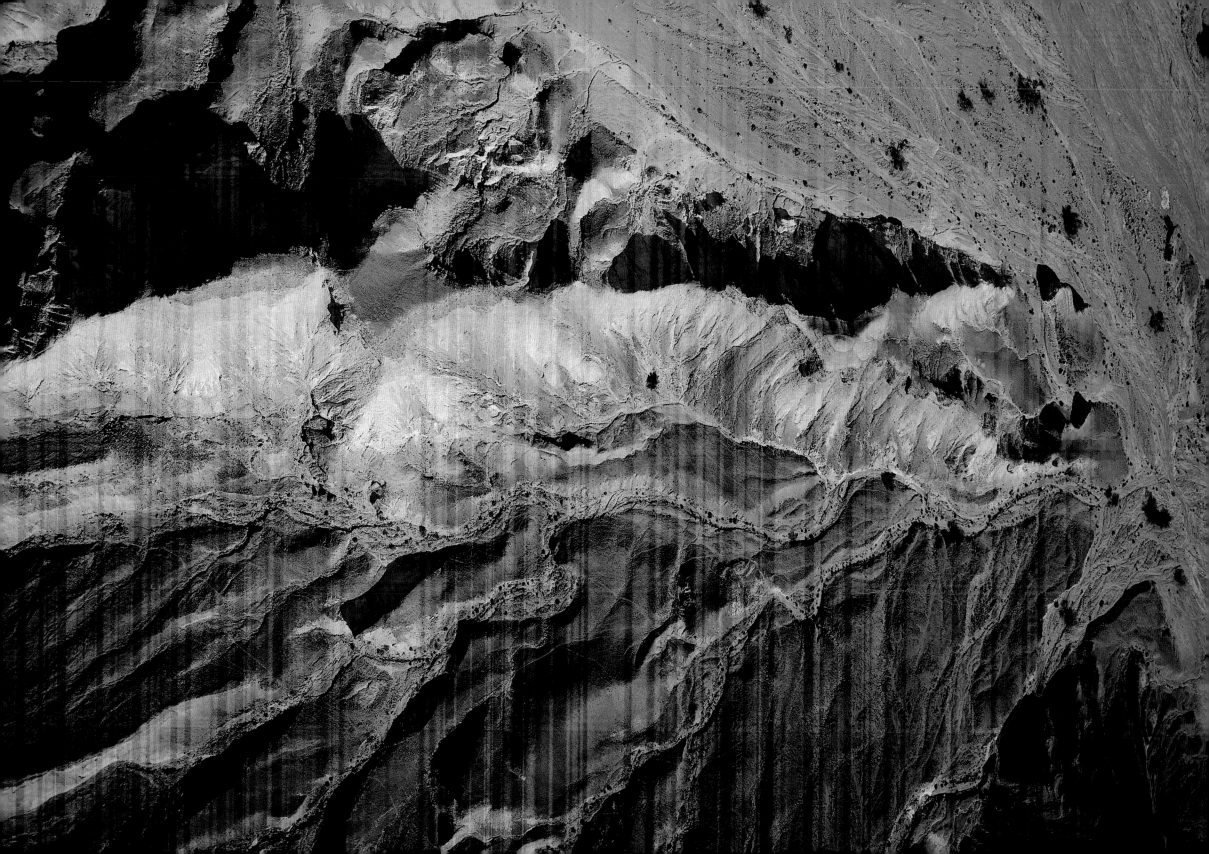

נחל כרכם
Karkom wadi

הר כרכם
Mt. Karkom

הר כרכם
Mt. Karkom

נחל כרכם
Mt. Karkom

נחל פארן והר כרכם במערב
Paran wadi.
Mt. Karkom on the west

159

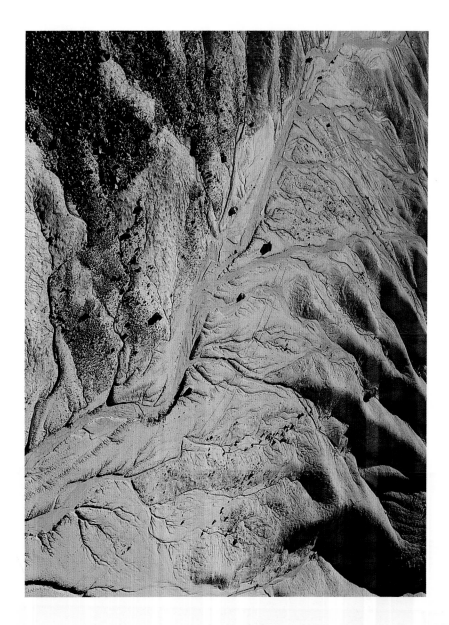

נחל המש‍ר
Hameshar wadi
◇
מורדות הר צוריע‍ז
Mt. Zuri'az slopes

נחל אשל והר צוריעז

Eshel wadi & Mt. Zuri'az

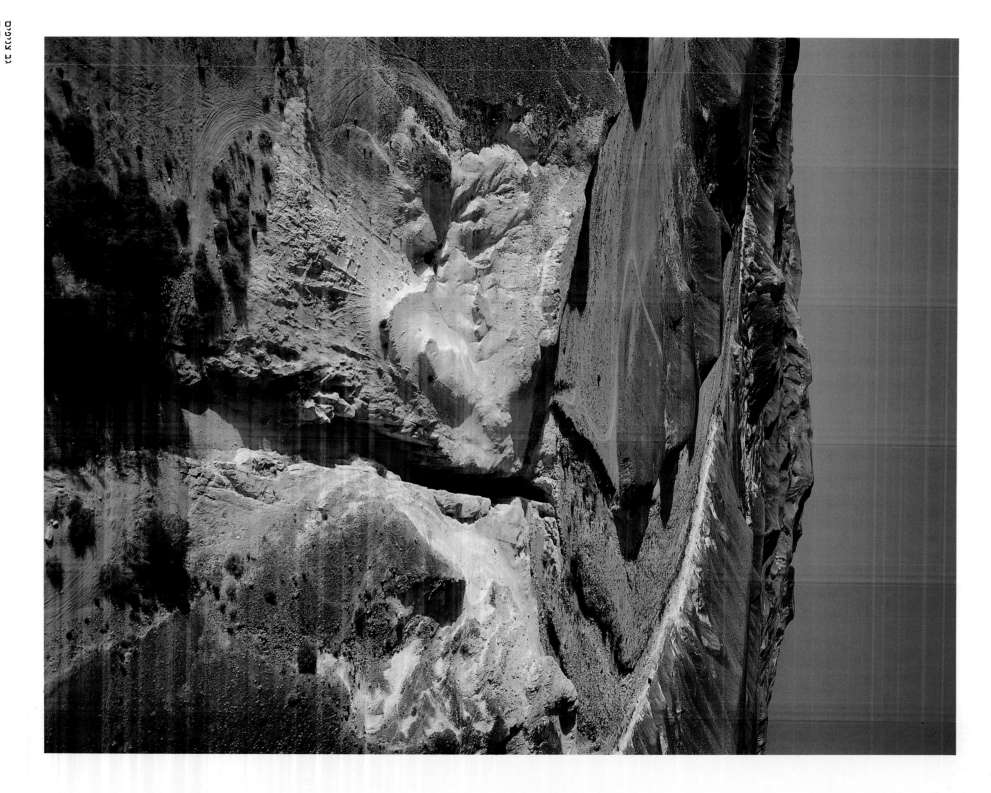

גב צניפים
Zenifim waterhole

באר עדה ונחל פארן
Ada well & Paran wadi

הקניון הלבן ונחל שגיא
The white canyon
& Saggi wadi

150

נחל כרכום
Karkom wadi

התגליות הגדולות

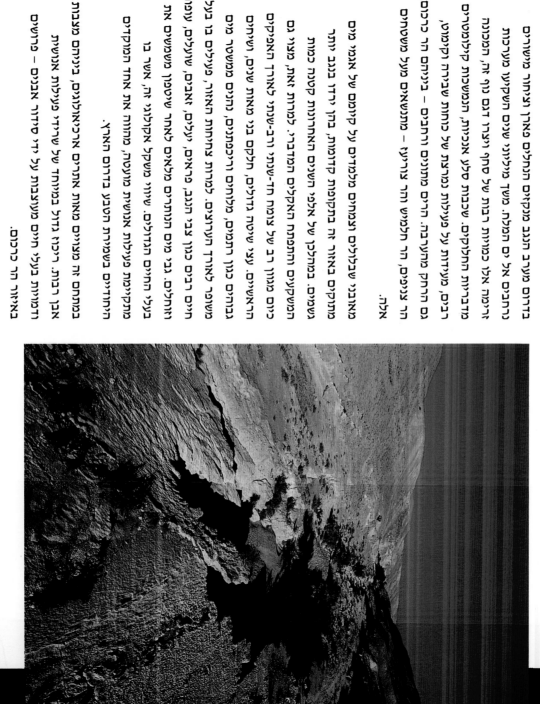

THE VALLEYS REGION

North of the Shani Wadi, the mountainous view is replaced by a plateau composed of light brown marine sedimentary rocks. Two large valleys are found in the elevated plateau area: the Uvda (100 sq.km.) and the Sayyarim (20 sq.km.). Both extend north and south, draining through the Hiyyon and Arava Wadis into the Dead Sea.

Archaeological excavations provide evidence that approximately 9,000 years ago man colonized this barren, arid area. Its first inhabitants were hunters who left behind dwelling places and campsites in which animal bones and flint utensils have been found.

Close to the year 5,000 B.C.E., ancient man became skilled in agricultural techniques. Remains of settlements containing some of the world's oldest threshing floors and a variety of agricultural equipment, testify to ancient man's remarkable ability to store water and cultivate the harsh desert terrain. Other archaeological evidence illustrate how gazelle hunters used stone walls called 'kites', as traps. Local armies and governments outfitted trade routes with way-stations and fortresses for copper-seeking Egyptians, who were subsequently followed by the Nabataeans, Romans, Byzantines and Muslims. Lastly, additional finds such as open temples and tombstones, point to man's religious inclinations, while campsites and rock carvings shed light on the life of travelling minstrels.

Until Israel's establishment, Bedouins grew grains along the Hiyyon River, making use of dams to control the water flow and prevent erosion. Golden sands, composed of minute fossils and gleaming grains of quartz, can be found north-east of the Uvda Valley. These magnificent dunes cover the entrances of the Kasui and Yitro wadis as well as wadi edges.

דיונת הכסוי
Kasuy dune

145

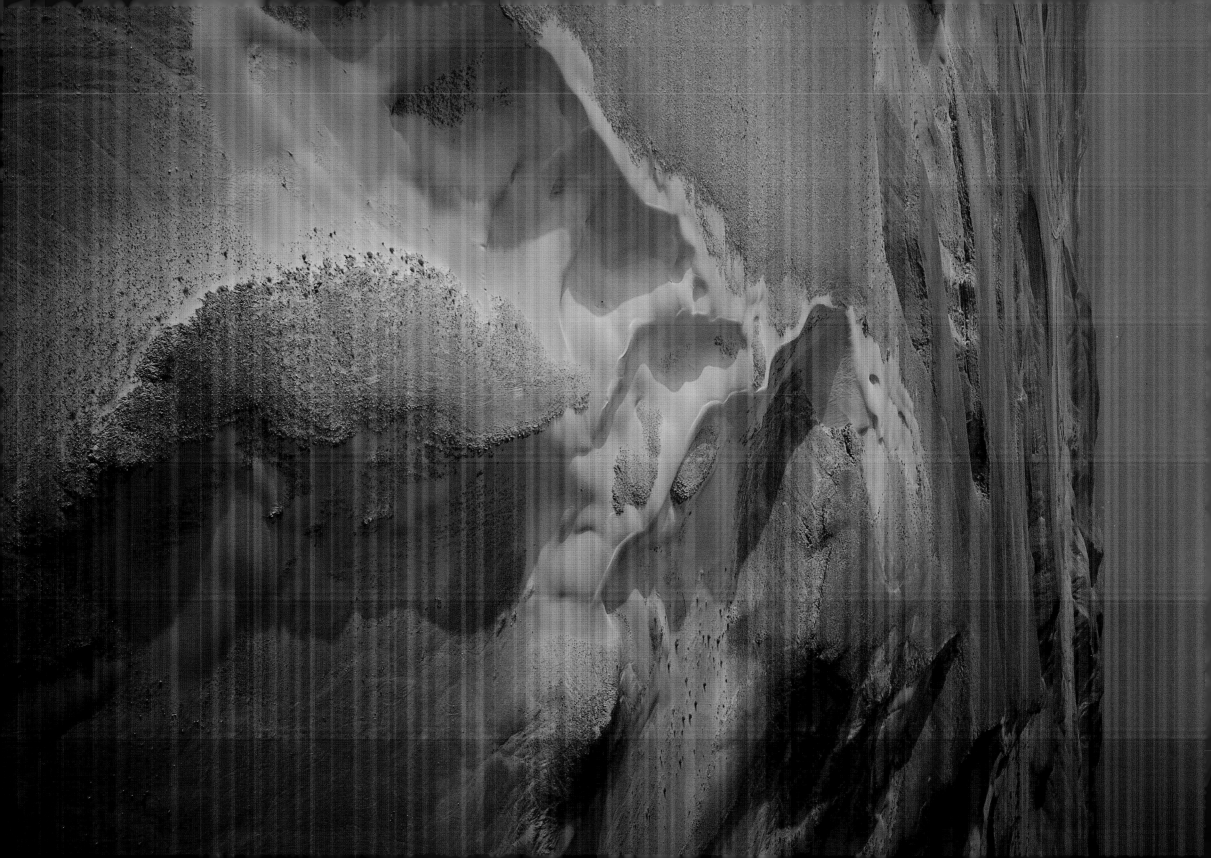

נחל רחם, ויובלים עליונים, מבט דרומה
Upper streams of Raḥam wadi, a southern view

עמוד סלע מצפון לקניון האדום
A pillar
north of the red canyon

נחלי בותם
Botem wadi strams

מדרונות הר עתק, מבט מהמזרח
Mt. Eteq slopes. an eastern view

הר עתק
Mt. Eteq

נחל רחם, יובלים עליונים, מבט דרומה
Upper streams of Raḥam wadi, a southern view

נחל עתק
Eteq wadi

דיונה בשולי נחל יתרו
A dune on the edge
of Yitro wadi

דיונת הכסוי
Kasuy dune

133

דיונת הכסוי
Kasuy dune
◊
נחל יתרו
Yitro wadi

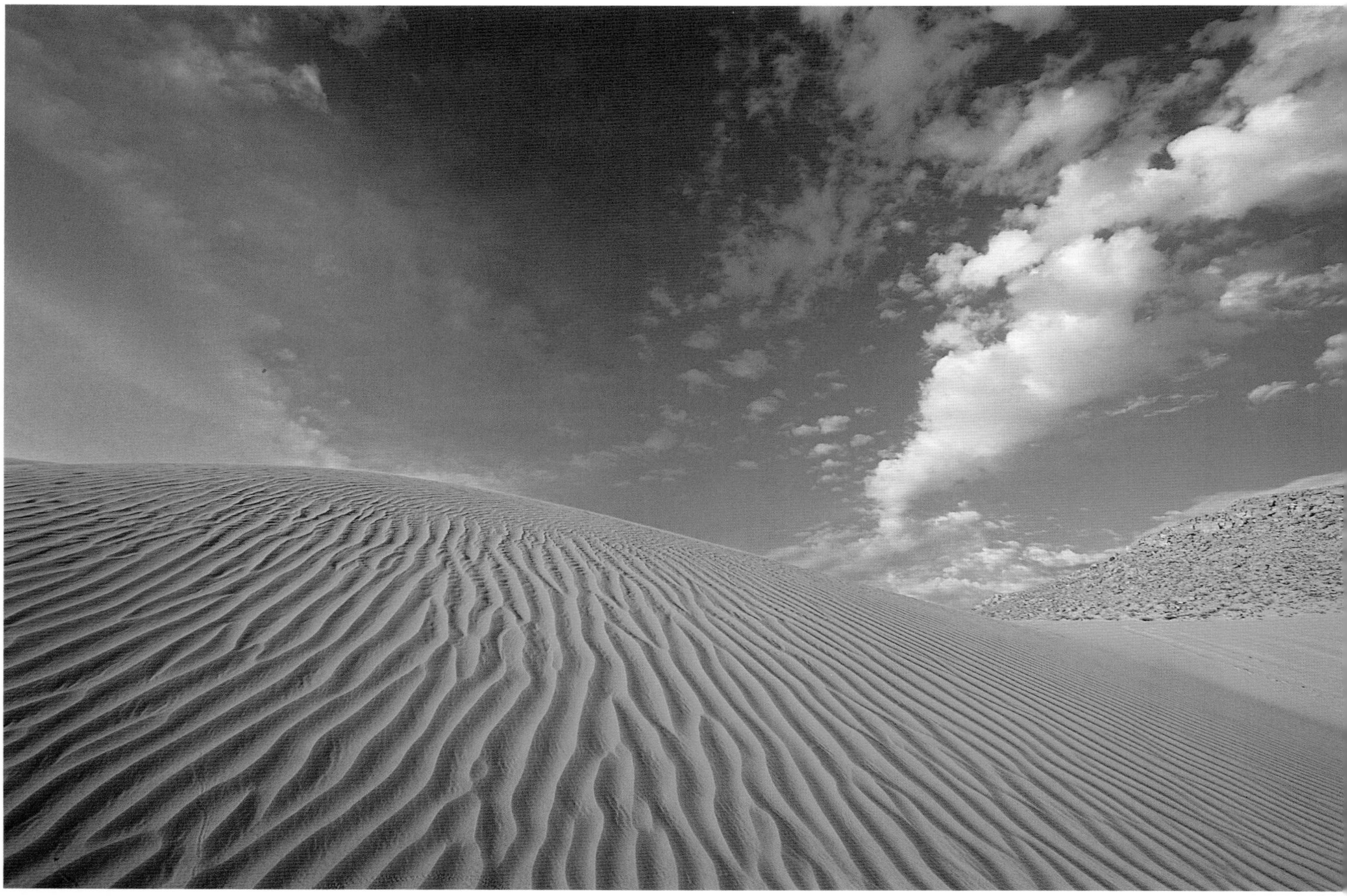

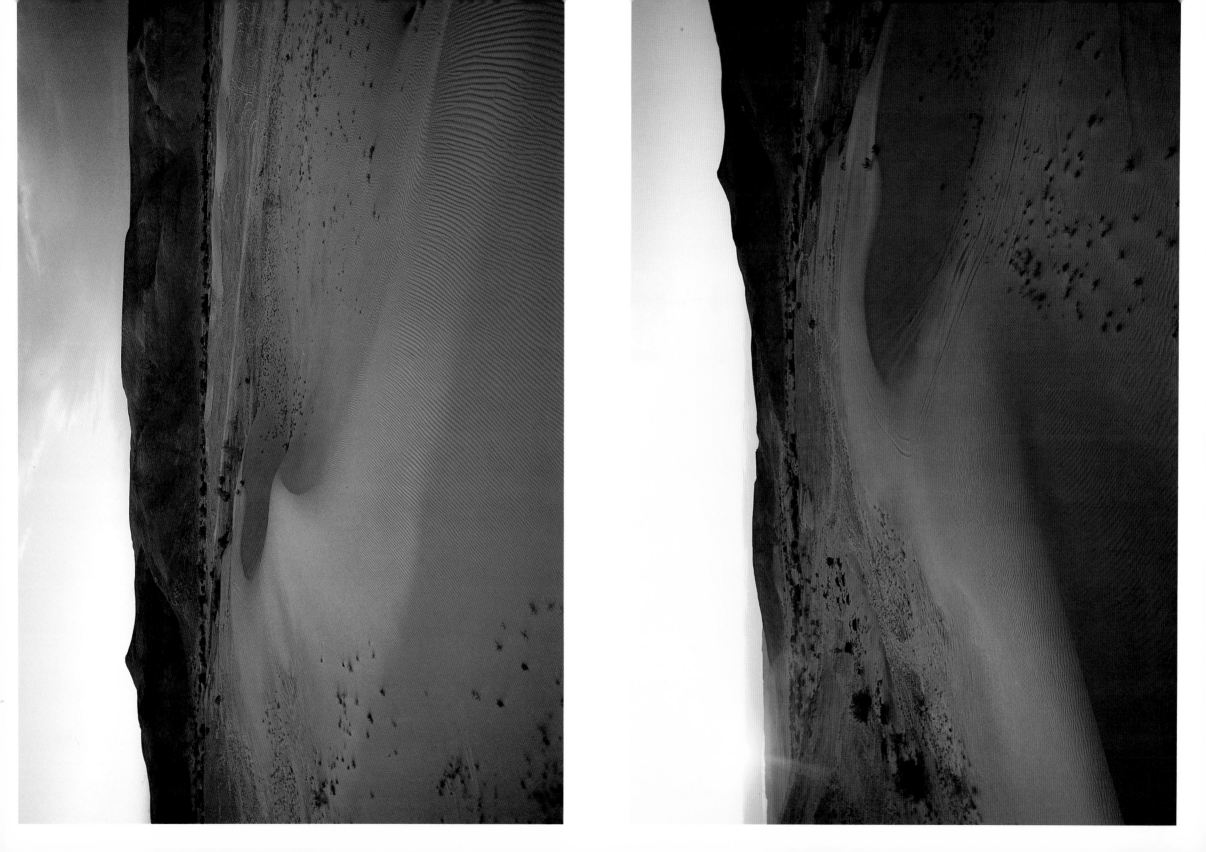

נחל כסוי
Kasuy wadi

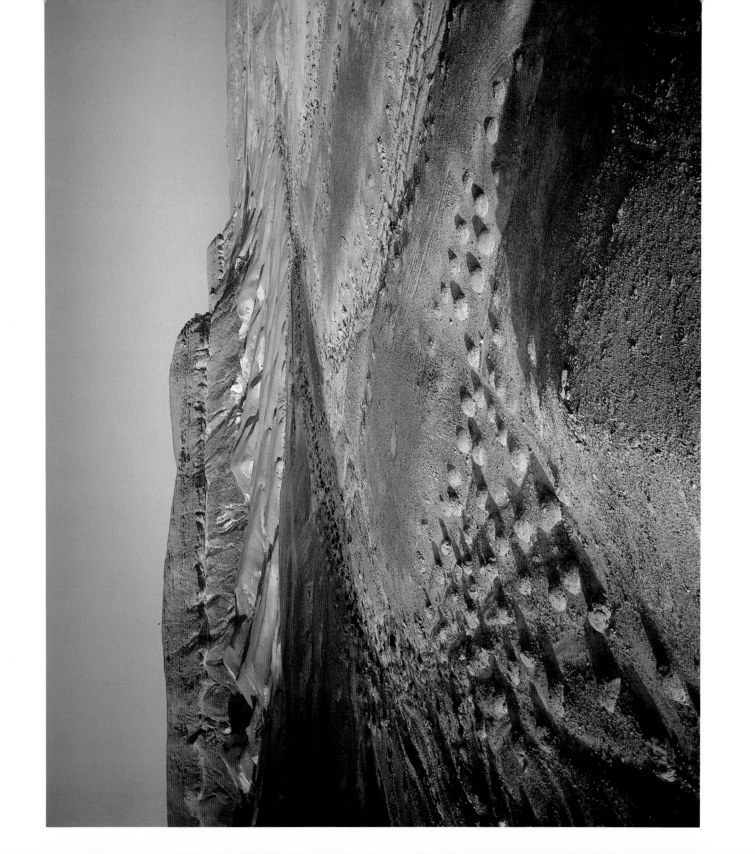

בצלים בבקעת סייארים

Bulbs in Sayyarim valley

129

אתרי בקעת עובדה
Uvda valley sites

ציורי אבן בבקעת עובדה
Uvda valley rock engravings

אזור נחל גרזי
Girzi wadi area

אזור נחל גרזי, מבט דרומה
Girzi wadi area, a southern view

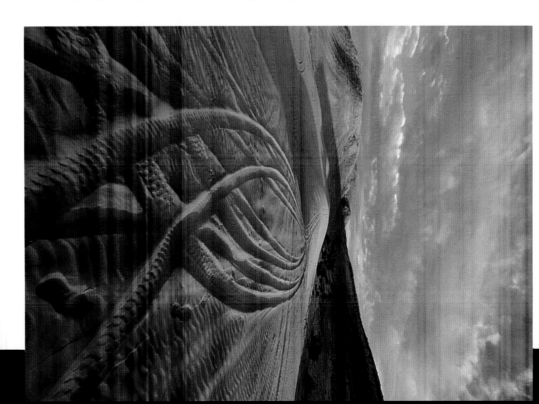

אזור הקאסוי

לוטן
Lotan

שחרות
Sha<u>h</u>arut

יהל
Yahel

נאות סמדר
Neot Smadar

נחל שיטים
Nahal shittim

נווה חריף
Newe Harif

EILAT MOUNTAINS

Israel's magical Eilat region offers a variety of spectacular mosaical views. The area's elementary and sedimentary rocks reveal a fascinating geological history. In fact, Eilat is the only region in Israel where granite rocks, remarkable for their deep red hues, exist. The creation of these rocks can be traced back 550 million years ago when the earth quaked in turmoil, creating a new geological order.

Eilat's granite mountains are bordered by an accumulation of sandstones which sunk into river beds. The Red Canyon and the Amram Pillars are examples of winding channels and columns carved out of sandstone through erosion.

The layered, light colored rocks are marine sedimentary rocks enriched by fossils. Over the centuries, the earth's restlessness caused geological fractures in the Arava Valley and in the Gulf of Eilat. As a result, geological layers were distorted and mountainous protuberances appeared.

From an aerial view, dark and light alternating strips can be seen stretching from south to north. This mix is a result of old elementary rock erosion found in Mt. Shelomo, Mt. Jehoshaphat and other sites. Between them, relatively new marine sedimentary rocks were preserved, as witnessed in Mt. Yo'ash and Givat Rehav'am.

To the east, the Eilat mountains are bordered by the Arava Valley and the Gulf of Eilat. The lunar valley dominates the western expanse. Meanwhile, northern borders are flanked by the peaks of Mt. Neshef and Mt. Shani, which reach 900 meters.

נחל עמרם
Amram wadi

121

נחל שחורת
Sheḥoret wadi area

מוצא נחל עמרם
Amram wadi outlet

◊

נחל שחורת
Sheḥoret wadi area

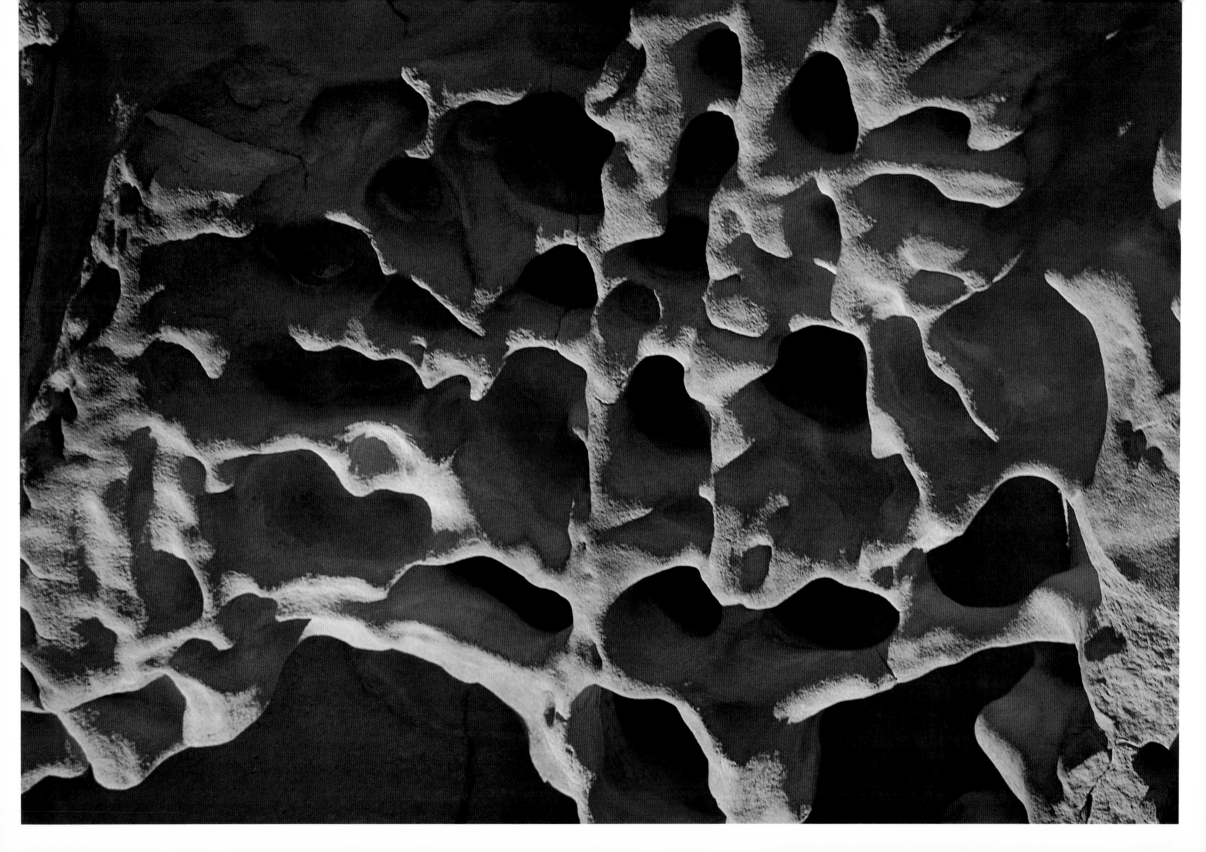

אתר פסל בארי "הפסלים" בנחל אמר
Sculptures wadi, near Be'er Ora

נחל עמרם
Amram wadi

נחל רחם
Raḥam wadi

הר שחורת, מבט לדרום מזרח
Mt. Sheḥoret, a southeastern view

הר אמיר, מבט לצפון
Mt. Amir, a northern view

הר אמיר, מבט לדרום מזרח
Mt. Amir,
a southeastern view

בעיר הרבעם וחופשי, מבט צפונה
Reḥav'am hill & Mt. Yohoshaphat

מעלה כבש אילת, מבט דרומה
Ma'ale Eilat,
an eastern view

הר אמיר, מבט מזרחה

Mt. Amir, an eastern view

109

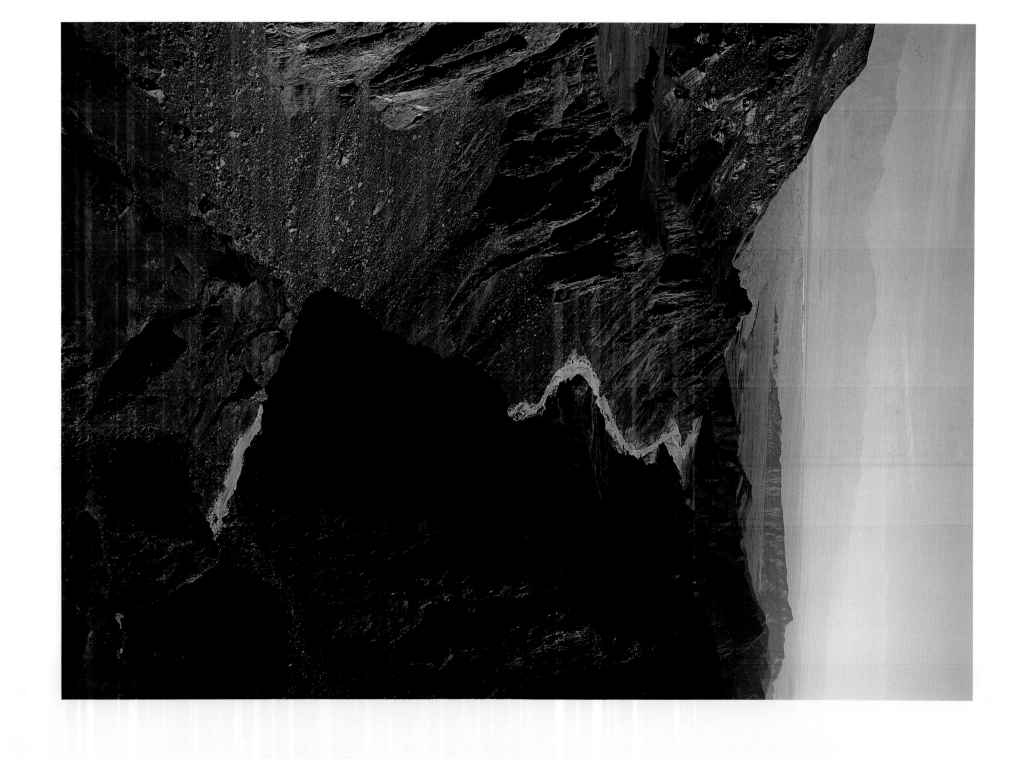

נחל צפונית, מבט לכיוון דרום־
מזרח
Ẕfunot wadi,
a southeastern view

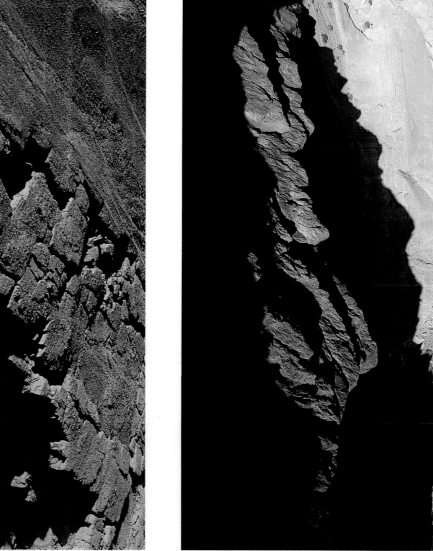

הר שלמה
Mt. Shelomo

סדקי שחורת
Sheḥoret fissures

נחל שחורת
Sheḥoret wadi

גבעת הרחבעם, מבט דרומה
‏∿‏
Rehav'am hill, a southern view

צוקי גישרון, מבט דרומה
‏∿‏
Gishron's cliffs,
a southern view

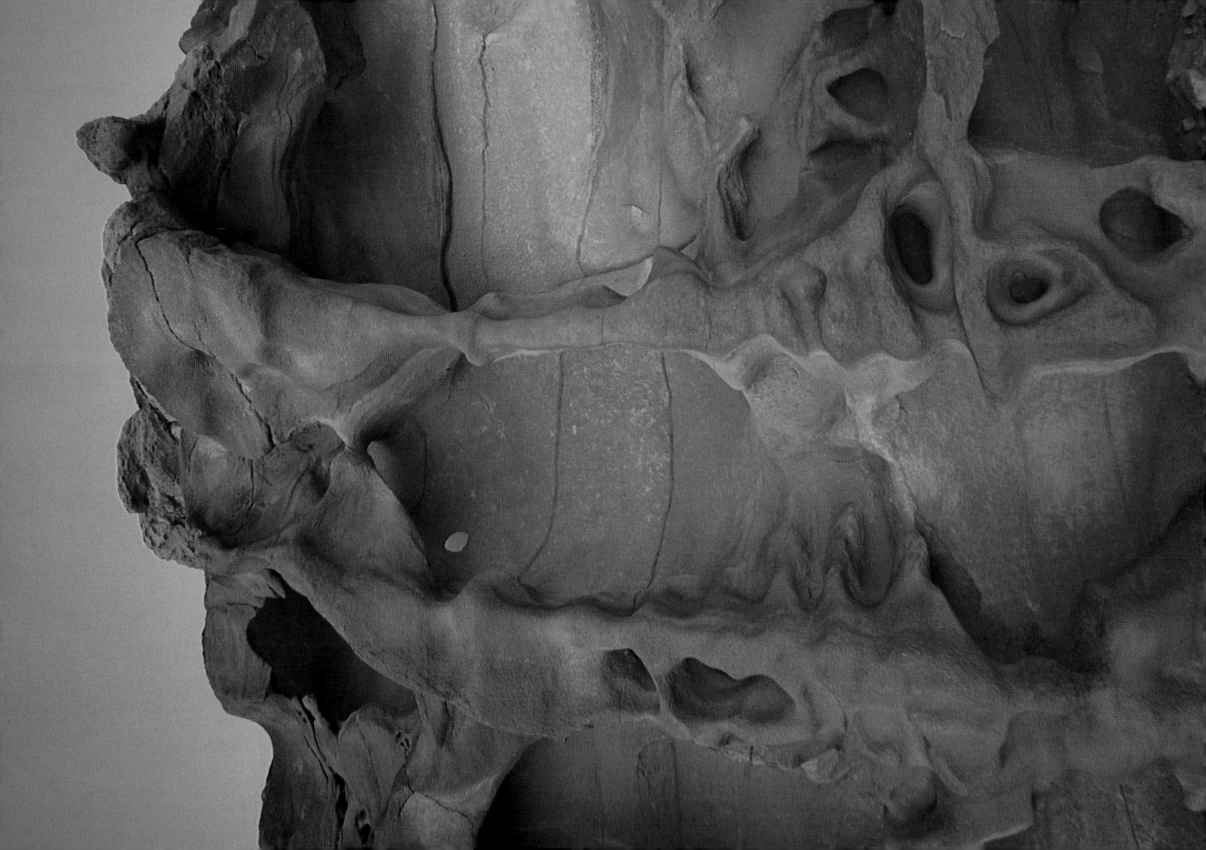

הר אילת

פסלים בנחל ליד באר אורה
Sculptures wadi, near Be'er Ora

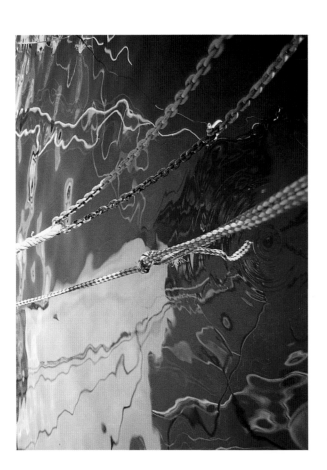

EILAT

Today, Eilat is a modern, bustling city of 35,000 residents, yet its history can be traced back to the Bible. It first appears in the Scriptures describing Israel's arduous journey from Egypt to the Promised Land (Deuteronomy II:viii).

Towards the end of Israel's War of Independence the region was conquered by Negev-Palmach and Golani brigades. On March 10, 1949, 'Operation Uvda' concluded with an Israeli victory flag flying over Um-Rashrash. The following year Shahal volunteers joined the group of soldiers who had settled the area.

In March of 1950, the cornerstone of Eilat's first fifty apartments was laid. Eilat remained under military rule until the introduction of the local council in 1952. During that same year, plans for building Eilat's Port were announced. In 1955, the city inaugurated its first school. Two years later marked another first – the opening of the 'Eilat Hotel'. In 1959, the oil pipe which stretched between Eilat and Beer Sheva was extended to Haifa. That March, Eilat celebrated its tenth anniversary and was officially declared a city.

1963 was marked by the creation of a copper company named 'Timna' which became the city's main source of employment. The worldwide drop in copper prices resulted in the cessation of mining and the firing of hundreds of Eilat's citizens. In 1965, Eilat's new port was finally opened. Its operation reached its peak in the 1970's when Iranian oil was imported through it, as well as a variety of goods coming from the Third World. Following the Suez Canal reopening the port lost its economic and political clout. Today, the Eilat port operates at a reduced level and is mainly used for importing Japanese cars and oil produced in the Gulf of Suez. Chemicals manufactured in the Negev and Dead Sea are sent through the Eilat Port to Africa and countries in the Far East.

Tens of thousands of sea, sun and desert seeking foreign and Israeli tourists come to Eilat every year. The Israel-Egypt peace accord, direct charter plane air routes to and from Europe, and the ASTA Free Trade Agreement have led to an unprecedented growth in tourism. With the realization of Israeli-Jordanian-Egyptian peace, the region is bound to become one of the Middle East's central attractions over the coming years.

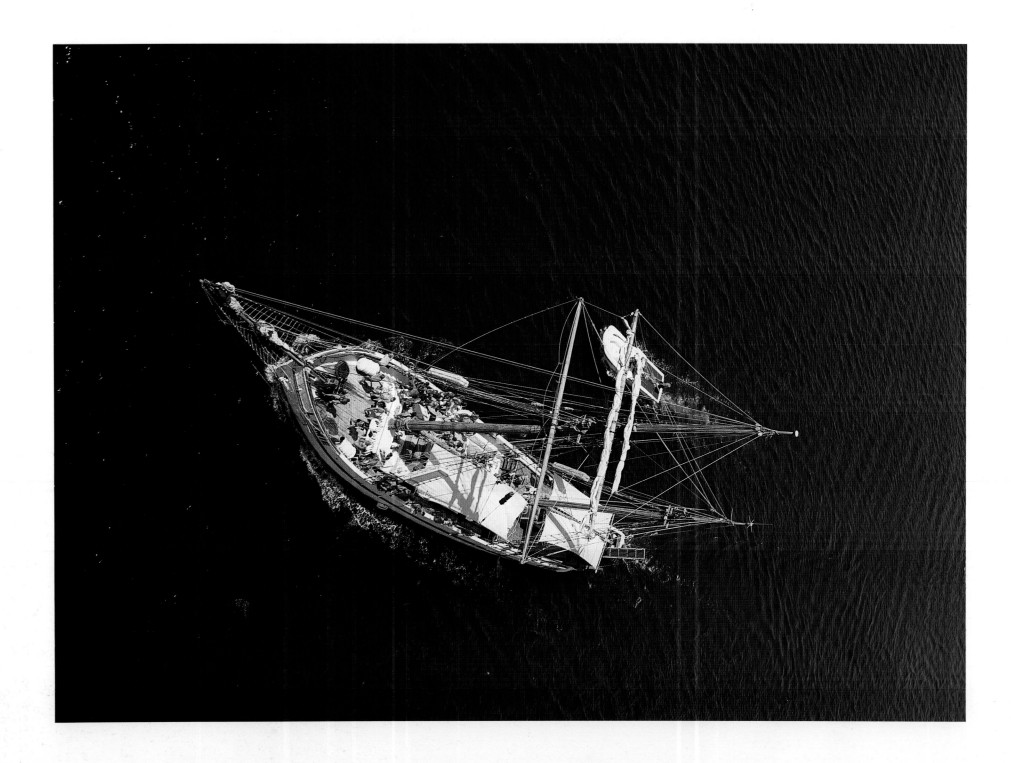

אילת, מבט מזרחה

Eilat, an eastern view

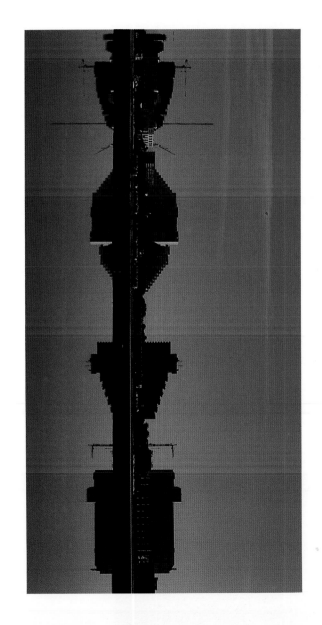

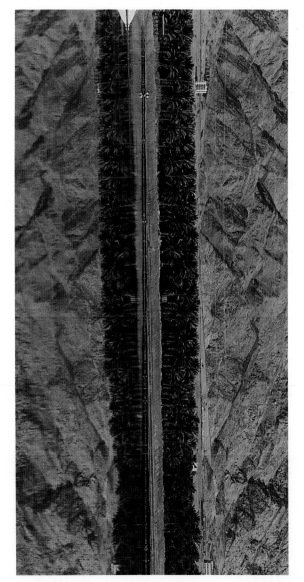

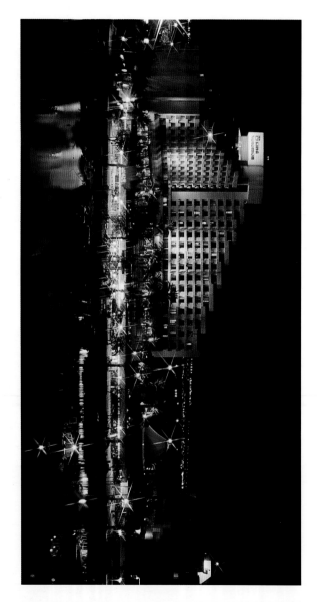

התצפית התת-ימי
Eilat, underwater observatory

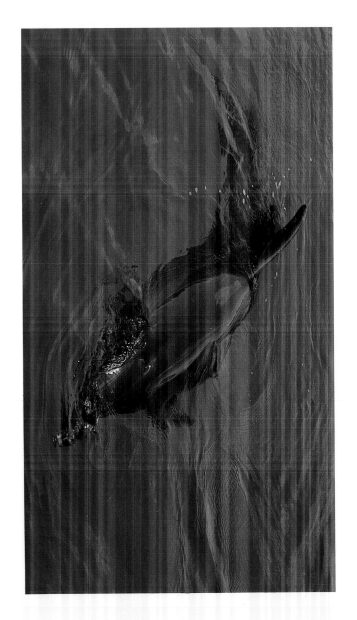

אילת

אילת, חוף אלמוגים
Eilat, Coral beach

TIMNA VALLEY

Timna Valley offers a wide variety of breathtaking views, as well as archaeological and geological sites of international importance. The valley is a geological window revealing both white and colorful sandstones which create a unique landscape, characterized by Solomon's Pillars, the stone Mushroom and several majestic arches.

The valley's famous rocks contain a wealth of minerals. Copper, the first metal produced by man, was originally discovered and produced in Timna over 7,000 years ago. Various methods of extracting copper from rocks were eventually developed, first by means of stone hammers, later by bronze chisels.

Timna is the oldest mining site in the world. Ancient mines and smelting sites can still be seen. Timna's work camps, dwelling sites, altar remains and wall drawings reveal a wide range of human activities which peaked during the Egyptian period, some 3,200 years ago. After the state of Israel was founded, copper mining and production was renewed, requiring the use of large open mines as well as subterranean mines several kilometers long. Every year close to a million tons of rocks were mined, out of which ten thousand tons of copper were extracted. Through the use of chemicals, metal was separated from rocks and used to make electric cables, coins and military equipment. In 1984, mining ceased, resulting in large mounds of lead on the edges of Timna Valley.

תמנע. עמודי שלמה

Timna. Shelomo pillars

בקעת ספגון והר מכרות
Sasgon hill & Mt. Mikhrot

הר תמנע וקבוץ אליפז
Mt. Timna & kibbutz Elifaz

72

הקשת
The arch

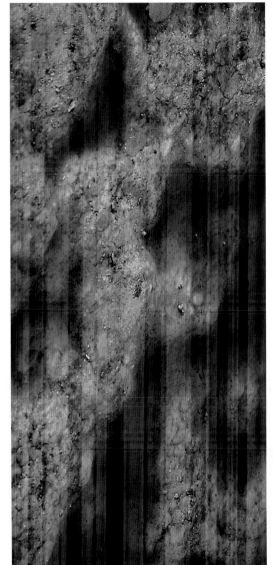

מפעל הנחושת בתמנע
Timna copper plant

נחל נחושתן, יובלים עליונים
Neḥushtan wadi, upper streams

נחל נחושתן
Neḥushtan wadi

בקעת תמנע
Timna valley

הפטרייה
The Mushroom

61

ארץ

בבקעות וצדק בתוכנו ובין הגרים, ובפרט כלפי אלה שאינם אזרחים, בעלי מעמד עראי או בכלל נטולי מעמד וזכויות כאזרח, היא אבן הבוחן של חברותנו.

נהוגים אנו לומר: ארץ ישראל.

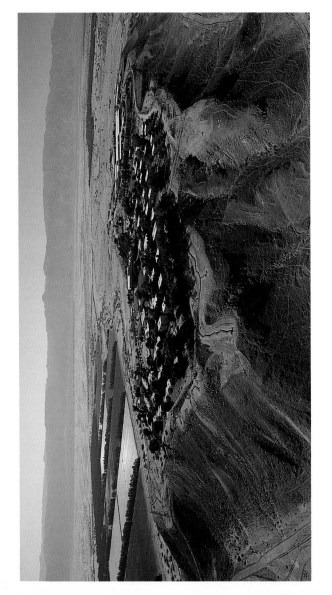

גרופית
Gerofit

סמר
Samar

אליפז
Elifaz

אילת
Eilot

יטבתה
Yotvata

קטורה
Qetura

THE SOUTHERN ARAVA

The southern Arava lies in the heart of the Syrian-African Rift, nestled between the Gulf of Eilat and the Noz_a Range. To the east stand the Edom mountains, looming over a thousand meters high. To the west, the fault escarpment, representing the water line between the Arava and the Negev. Fan-shaped eroded land surfaces spread out from the mountains towards the center of the valley.

The Arava landscape is composed of wadi pebbles, sand dunes and salt playa – flat, sterile plains devoid of any vegetation. Rain water drains into the valley's low areas, such as Yotvata's playa, never reaching the sea. After heavy flooding, lakes appear in the salt bogs, only to evaporate within a few months' time.

Most of the Arava's flowing waters penetrate the earth, merging with salty ground water. Agricultural farms, like Evrona, have benefitted from this water supply.

Despite the Arava's history of raging, sweltering temperatures during a good part of the year, human activity can be traced as far back as 10,000 years ago. Today, local farmers have created a flourishing agronomy based on the harvest of dates,.mangos and pomelos. Notwithstanding harsh conditions, local kibbutzim have built thriving dairy farms. For instance, the emulsification performed at Yotvata dairies has yielded refreshing dairy products enjoyed country-wide. Still, the difficulties of desert agriculture combined with a continued kibbutz expansion prompted local inhabitants to seek their fortunes in other areas, such as tourism, industry and fish farming.

The Hai Bar wildlife preserve was built in the local salt playa. Several desert animals, including large herbivores, such as oryx, wild asses and ostriches, as well as small carnivores, such as sand foxes, mountain foxes, sand cats, wolves, hyenas, leopards, karakuls, and reptiles may be seen at Hai Bar. The Arava is a main route for migrating birds during the spring and autumn and the perfect bird-watching site for hundreds of thousands of charming songbirds, water fowl and imposing birds of prey journeying to a warmer climate.

הברכה בנחל רודד

A rain-pool at Roded wadi

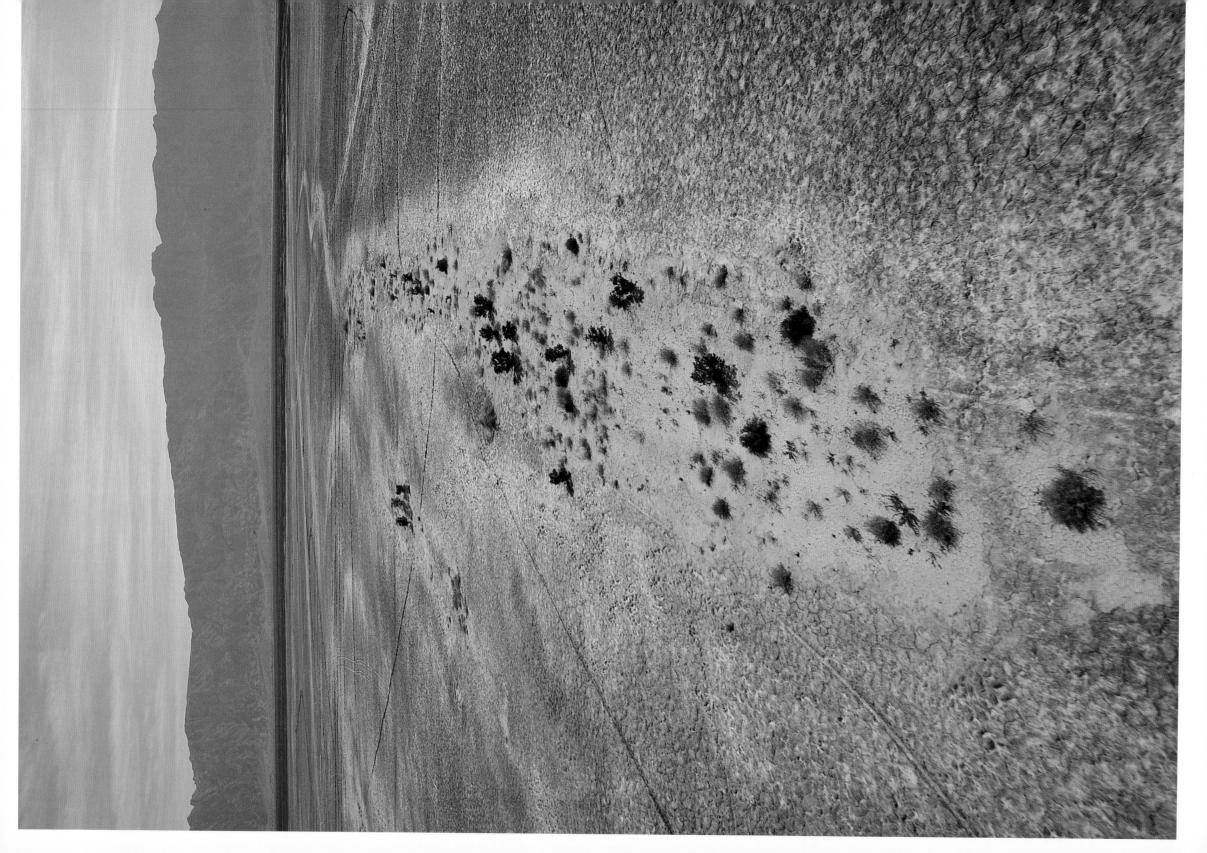

מלחת יוטבתה
Yotvata salina

נחל שעלב
Sha'alav wadi

שדות יטבתה
Yotvata fields

שדות אליפז
Elifaz fields

בולבוסים בהר שעלב
Bulbs at Mt.Sha'alav

חוות רודד
Roded farm

48

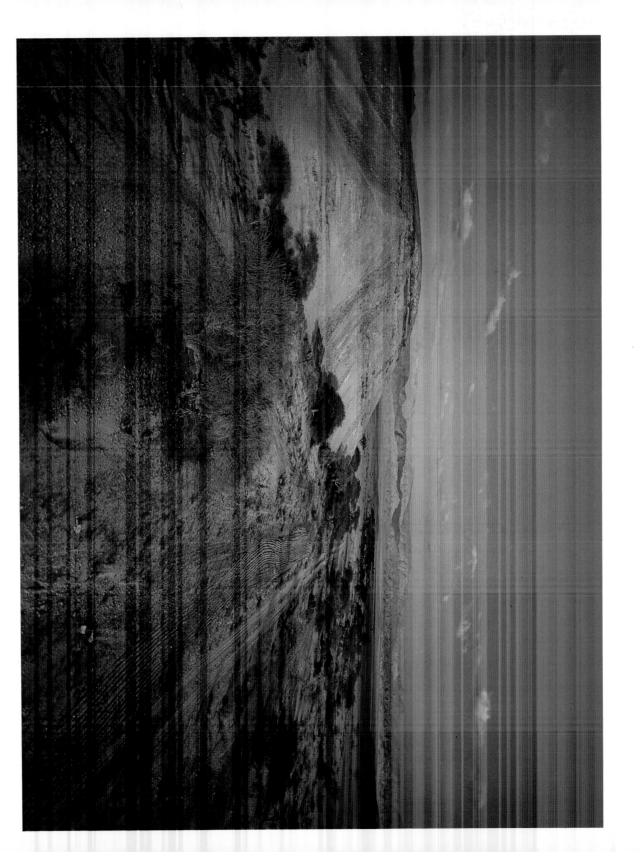

נחל יעלון וקבוץ יהל
Ya'alon wadi & kibbutz Yahel

נחל שיטה
Shitta wadi

46

מצוק העתקים מערבית ליטבתה
Fault escarpment, west of Yotvata

למרגלות הר קטורה
foot of Mt. Qetura

45

ברידה בנחל רודד
A rain pool at Roded wadi

חי בר
Yotvata reserve
(hay – bar)

42

צומת קטורה "הקיר"
Qetura junction "wall"

חולות סמר
Samar sands

40

חולות סמר

Samar sands

חולות סמר

Samar sands

37

בנחל רודד בריכת מי גשמים
A rain pool at Roded wadi

יטבתה, מטע תמרים
Yotvata. Palm plantation

35

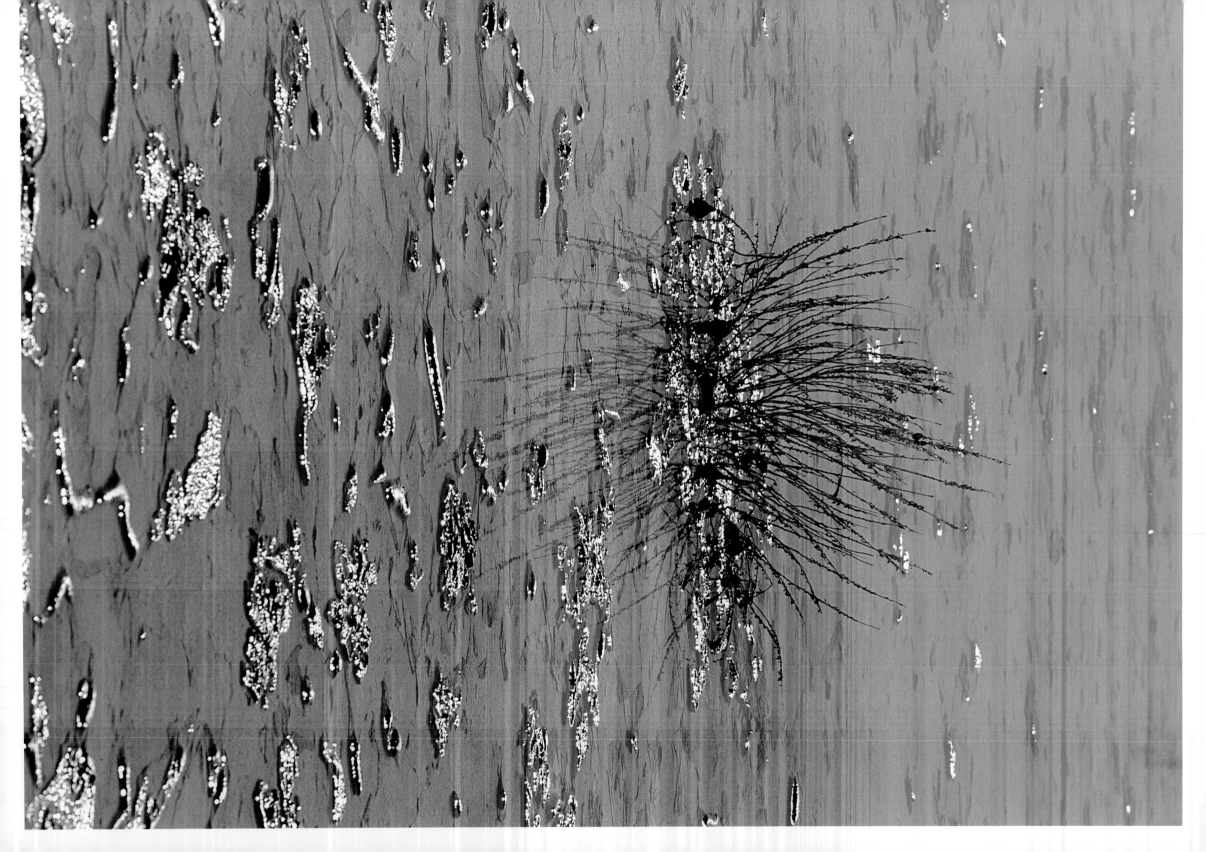

הדורה הדקל

קטורה, מטע תמרים
Qetura, palm plantation

ARAVA EDGES

Several sprawling plains stretch north of the Uvda Valley, flanked on the east by mountain ranges bordering the Arava Valley. Bracketing this area from the north, stands the Menuha Range. Various forms of vegetation prove the existence of water sources. Trees and perennial bushes grow only in river channels where large amounts of flood water accumulate, allowing plants to endure even in the driest of years.

From an airplane, it is possible to spot wadis by the concentration of vegetation. In wadis where the drainage basin is small, plants grow in the center of channels; while in wadis with bigger drainage basin, there are two lines, of plants.

In the spring when the annual flora bursts into a dazzling display of colors with the first torrential rainfall, the desert is transformed into a kaleidoscopic wonderland. The relatively modest blooming of plants, like Negev lilies and scarlet coronillas, only occurs in the spring and autumn.

After a sufficient amount of rain has fallen, it is possible to observe up close the fascinating pollination and germination processes in plants such as the edible Blepharis, Rose of Jericho and Asteriscus Pygmaeus.

The Eshet Reservoir, capable of holding 3.7 million cubic meters of water, is found along Arava wadi beds, adjacent to Be'er Menuha. These waters are often used for irrigation in local moshav settlements.

צוקי חדוד ונחל פארן

Haddud cliffs & Paran wadi

27

מוצא נחל ורדית לפארן
Vardit wadi outlet
to Paran
◇
מים חיי בנחל עשת
Eshet reservoir

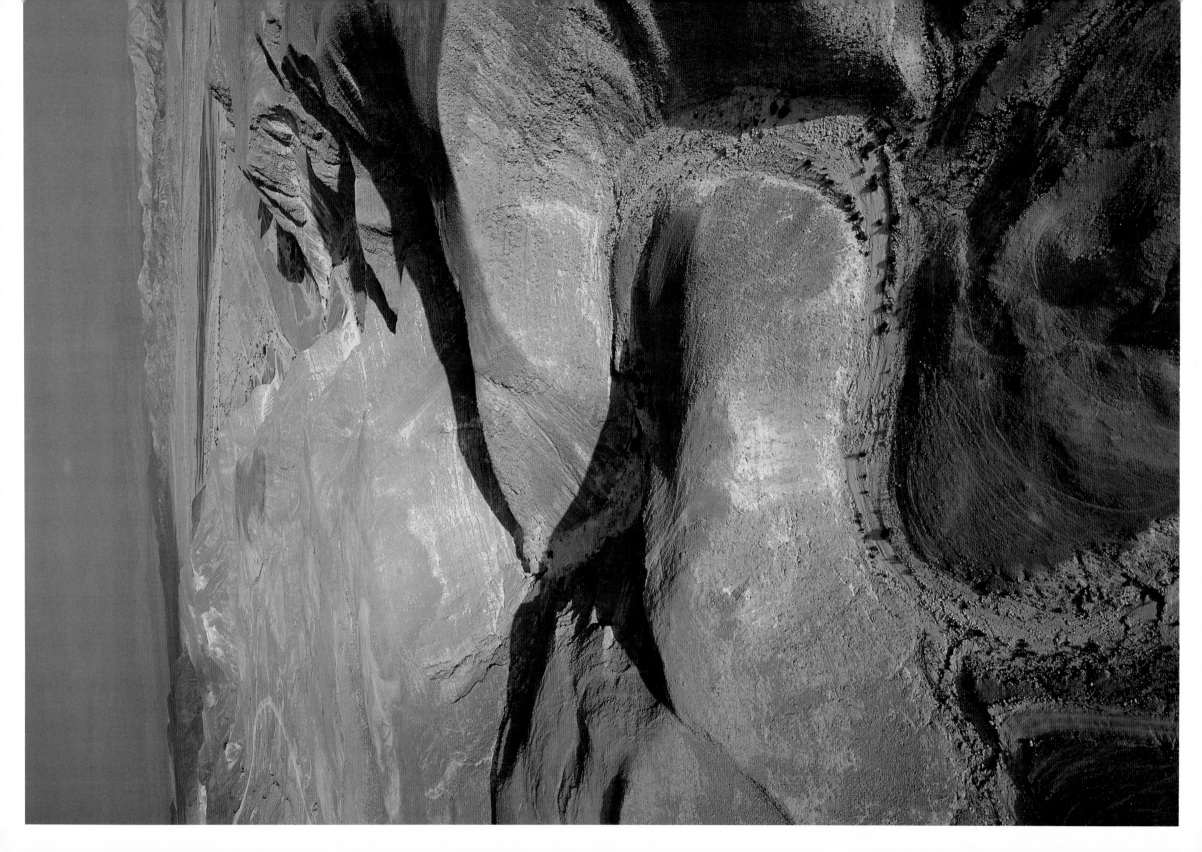

נחל ורדית
Vardit wadi

נחל ברק
Baraq wadi

24

מאגר עשת
Eshet reservoir

מוצא נחל ורדית לפארן
Vardit wadi outlet to Paran

גשר החיון בכביש הערבה
Hiyyon bridge
on the Arava road

22

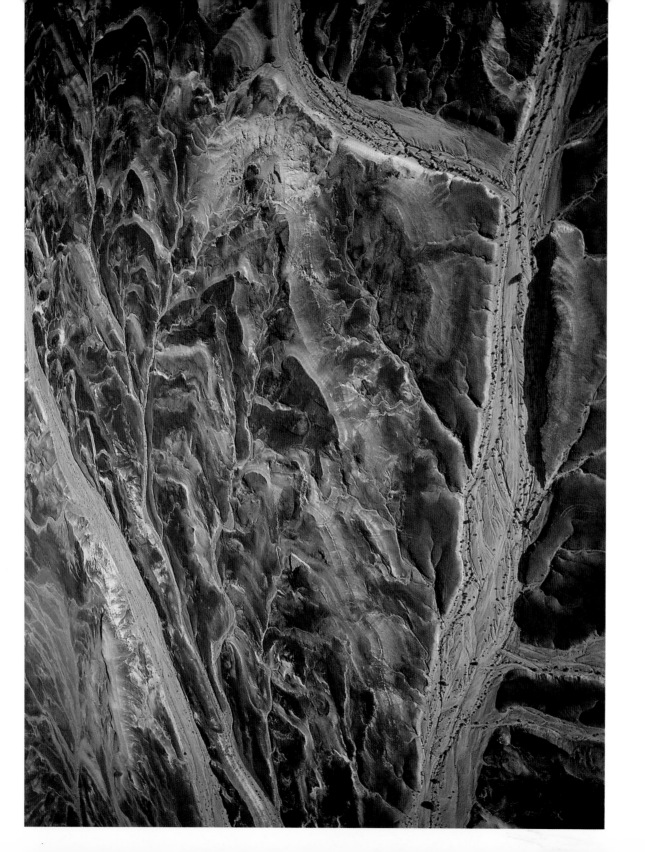

נחל חמדה
Hemda wadi

21

קרייתה בנחל שברים
Spring time
at Shevarim wadi

נחל פארן, מבט מזרחה
Paran wadi,
an eastern view

19

מאגר עשת
Eshet reservoir

נחל שברים ברכס מנוחה
Shevarim wadi
in the Menuẖa ridge

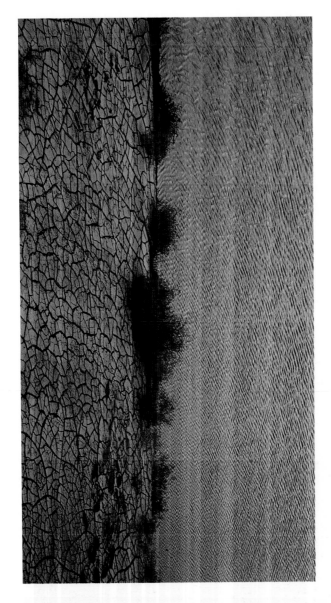

מאגר עשת

Eshet reservoir

16

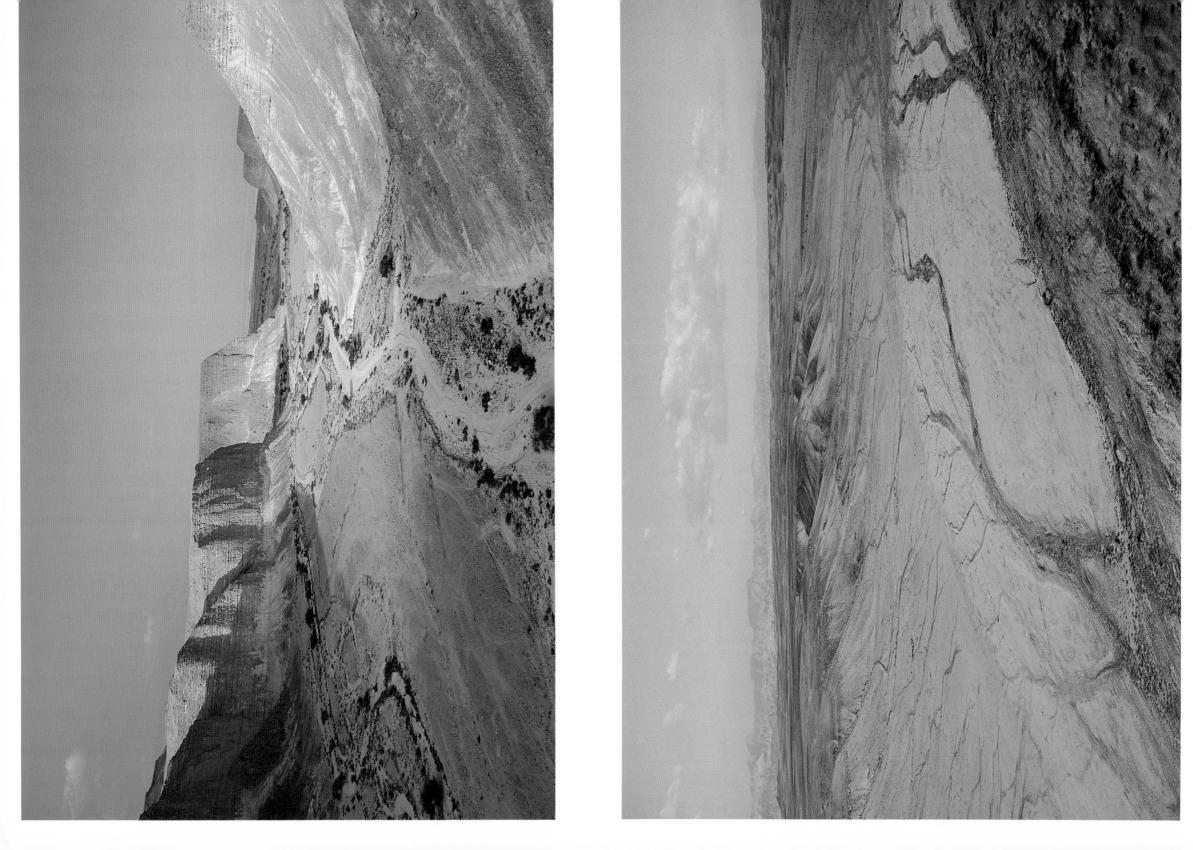

נחל ברק
Baraq wadi

נחל חיון
Hiyyon wadi

ליד החמדה ברכס מנוחה
Hemda hill, Menuḥa ridge

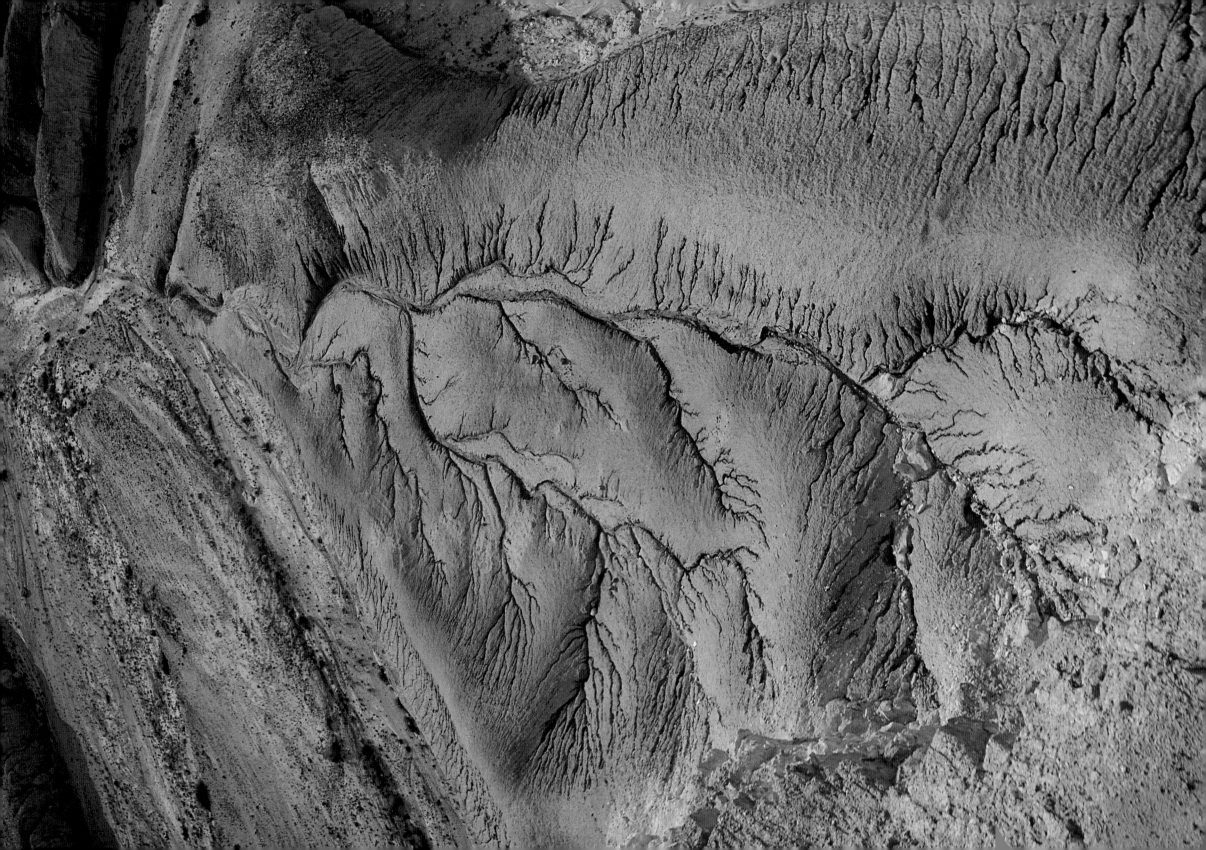

שלולי החמדה

אזור הר חמדה
Hemda hill area

פתח דבר

תוכן העניינים

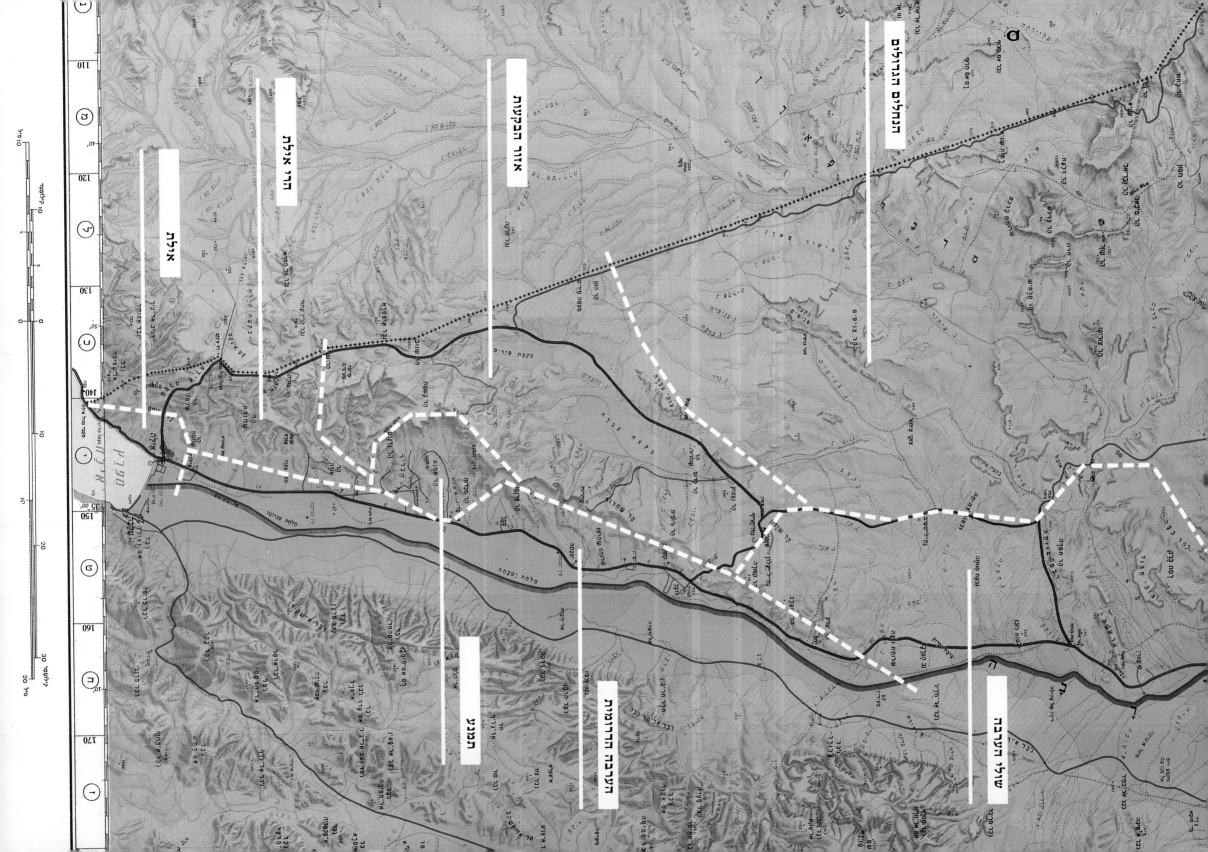

בצבע הסלע

ISBN 965-222-572-X

נדפס בישראל 1994

© Rohr Productions Ltd. C.N.E.S. 1994

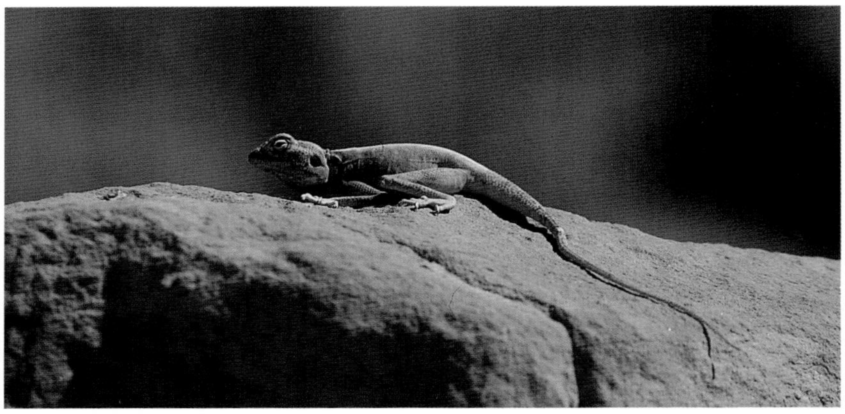

בקצה המדבר

קו האופק – חבל אילות

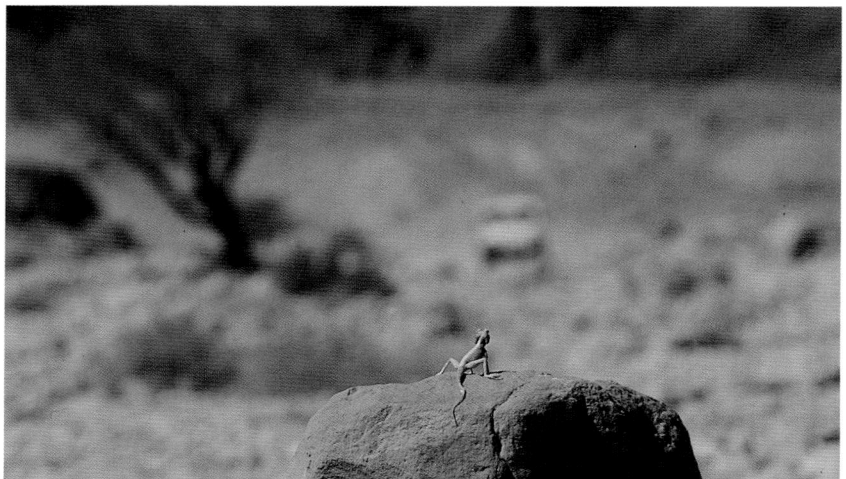